With *Ghetto Koans* James Cagney has his ear to the ground and his eyes wide open. An ode to Oakland, this collection speaks to the craziness one gets used to, and does so with surgical precision. Like the patient in "Overheard in the Dr's Office," each poem will have you hungry as a grave then, suddenly, just as sated.

—NICOLE SEALEY

In James Cagney's *Ghetto Koans*, visceral stories draw a map that guides the reader on a treasure hunt through the iridescent underside of a skewed society. Cagney's verses guide us through the littered streets of Oakland and beyond, where race and poverty dance a dark tango and "bullets are sperm fertilizing eggs in reverse." Here, dialogues emerge from tongues that speak the truths of God and of Patron, a wedding takes place in a basement Church, and a child named "The Rewarder of Thankfulness" flips and splits on an empty stage. Alive and incanting with poetic forms received, invented, inverted, enumerated into lists, and chanted into urban spells, Ghetto Koans is a "flower (that) cuts through the bullshit between people", snipped by "a ninja jingling with blades"—and true to its name, shows us the nature of reality, and leaves us feeling as though "wherever we were going, we had arrived already".

—MAW SHEIN WIN, author of *Storage Unit for the Spirit House*

James Cagney's poems cut like scalpels through romanticism and self-deception as he reveals moments and characters many of us would turn away from. Yet they are bursting with the energy and culture that keep us moving. Cagney is an urban lyricist of earthquake magnitude.

—JEW⎵ ⎵ ⎵OMEZ, author *Still Water*

I hesitate to call a book beautiful in these difficult times because beauty so often means the surrender of our consciousness, our need to confront the fuckery of the moment and the life we endure. James Cagney's *Ghetto Koans* is perhaps the exception. It confronts the plight of human existence with unparalleled lyric intensity making for a reading experience like no other. Dare I say it? Fuck yeah I'll say it. This is a beautiful work of art!

—TRUONG TRAN, author of *Book of the Other: Small in Comparison*

In his new collection *Ghetto Koans: A Personal Archive*, James Cagney shows us how an understanding of the modern koan requires a surrealist eye with a nod to a narcotic based frenzy just underneath the dissociation of everyday survival. Moments of grace and light punctuate deftly laid out hood settings. The poet chronicles a "gone" world that isn't really gone, still preserved by an Oakland which functions as its own museum of humanity. These are the tales of the forgotten, quiet hustlers...not con artists...but real, breathing, blue collar hustlers whose lives have been shoehorned into the influence industry against their own dreams. Cagney illuminates these lives "into cleanliness beneath a flagellating sun." In reinventing the koan he also reinvents the villanelle, letting the voices of Oakland, California, Texas and ultimately our future take over the poems inside, all while wrapped inside a loose formalism. In revolutionizing form and voice, Cagney, whose poetic gifts were already considerable, is showing us there is no roof on how high his voice can rise. We can only hope, for our sakes, that he continues this evolution, and that we are ready for it.

—PAUL CORMAN-ROBERTS, author of *Bone Moon Palace* and *19th Street Station, Vol. 2*

Ghetto Koans: A Personal Archive is a visceral collection that resonates and vibrates the soul. James Cagney's verses are like stones thrown into still water; they ripple through the reader's soul, forcing us to confront the beauty and brutality of our shared humanity. In these poems, I see a heart that listens deeply to the unspoken, and in the debris of forgotten corners, discovers the light of endless worlds. This is not just a collection; it is a meditation on survival, an ode to the untold, and an invitation to find poetry in every crack of the city's skin.

—TSHAKA CAMPBELL, Santa Clara County
Poet Laureate Emeritus

Ghetto Koans

A PERSONAL ARCHIVE

BLACK LAWRENCE PRESS

Black Lawrence Press

Executive Editor: Diane Goettel

Cover and Interior Design: Zoe Norvell

Cover Artwork: "Feel the Heat" by Hunter Blaze Pearson

Copyright © James Cagney

2025

ISBN: 978-1-62557-1-625

All rights reserved. Except for brief quotations in critical articles or reviews, no part of this book may be reproduced in any manner without prior written permission from the publisher: editors@blacklawrencepress.com

Published 2025 by Black Lawrence Press.

Printed in the United States.

in memory of

West Oakland's poet laureate

Reginald Lockett

koan: (n.) (orig. Japanese) a paradoxical story, dialogue, question, or statement meditated upon to train Zen Buddhist monks to abandon dependence on reason and to force them into gaining sudden intuitive enlightenment.

TABLE OF CONTENTS

Preface {a closed library} ___ 1

Lemme Holla At You ___ 2

Untied ___ 4

Ultraviolet ___ 6

Solitary Dawn, Quarantine City ___ 7

Moment Of Silence ___ 8

U Get Used 2 The Craziest Shit ___ 9

Nigga Lover ___ 12

The Last Time I Pulled Over To Ask For Directions ___ 15

When They Rollback Prices On Yo Mama's Soda ___ 17

Sandwich School ___ 20

Overheard In Dr. Tim's Office ___ 21

Where U Try'n 2 Go? ___ 22

Gold Flip Flops & Sunflower Seeds ___ 25

Tina Turner's Wig Gives Its Final Public Address ___ 26

Beautician's Son ___ 28

Clothesline ___ 29

What Zero Sounds Like (After Watching Teenagers Attempt To Use A Rotary Phone) ___ 32

Three Variations ___ 37

Benjamin's Witnesses ___ 39

Preface To A Photograph: 1976 ___ 41

Worm's Easter Sunday Monologue ___ 43

Easter Weekend, Miami ___ 45

Flirting Phlebotomists ___ 46

Marquis ___ 48

Paychecks and Balances ___ 51

Dave's Wedding ___ 54

The Florist ___ 57

Bonfare: Fine Food Fast ___ 59

The Only Child ___ 61

Man-Talk ___ 63

Scars ___ 67

Ghost Homies ___ 68

Nobody Wants To Hear What God Has To Say About Love ___ 69

Bus Transfer ___ 73

The Boy In The ROTC Uniform ___ 74

Donate To The Crazy Fund ___ 77

A Blues From The Book Of Bob ___ 79

A Family Dinner In Berkeley ___ 82

Ideas of Home ___ 85

Housequake ___ 87

Commonalities ___ 89

This Past Saturday At Farmer's Market ___ 92

Acknowledgments ___ 97

About the author ___ 98

                    a closed library
                    a frightened animal
                    a captive audience

                    locusts hatching

                    a construction
mishap obscene phone call from the state

capital   ordained hobos + a missed train.

the moon swells, shattering the horizon like a plate

a bemused raccoon chews our list of rules to ribbons

                              solar eclipse   misdiagnosed
as high fever
                laid-off concubines in bright red collapse

                    city in crisis

LEMME HOLLA AT YOU
City Hall, _____

this city is in between cities right now
this city with dirty streets like collapsed arteries
this city is going through some things
and: *Just Can't* and: *Might Have To Be Put Down*

this city is where the rich compete in buildings
tagging territories with titanium graffiti

God being a poor man's investment
this city keeps its churches locked
open by request for those who tithe
more than used needles

this city closed its homeless shelters
for lack of corporate sponsors

at last night's news conference
the mayor broke out in tears
after someone stole the catalytic converter out of her limo
she admitted: the game has been rigged for decades,
but it's over now, baby

a skyline of empty buildings: fish tanks souped
with dead mollies

sunset sticks its fangs into skyscrapers
and sucks out the staff infection

from 98 floors up, the homeless smell fine
drug addicts can't be recognized
crawling like ants to shoot up
in the lobbies of buildings named after their grandparents

half the unhoused in heroin microsleep
own the properties where they're hosed off the entryway

this city is a dystopian movie set
and scaring the neighbor's gingerdoodle

the streets walk themselves grinding their teeth all night

the bridges are syringes
the sidewalk a belt knotted on a dead arm
this city is on the nod

this city stares at the moon unsure of its intentions
says, don't I know you from somewhere
says, *lemme hold onto a little somethingsomething*
before the next eclipse

no one will look this city in the eye
this city says everything's fine
this city will rise from the ashes of the suburbs and dance
just you watch from the cemetery

UNTIED
The Mouth, various

the tongue as knife, as grenade,
as pilot light to volcano

the tongue as butterfly shrapnel
      spraying radioactive glass

the tongue as battering ram,   axe handle,
desecrated cross, trigger

the tongue as begging puppy,
      as monster truck,
the tongue russian-neck-tied for a joke

the tongue as assassin: a ninja jingling with blades
cross-stepping the grassy knoll

the tongue as wooden stake, silver bullet,
      an earthquake with lightning in its hair

the tongue begging kryptonite to freebase

the tongue as apple,   and serpent   rolling
      its jellied eggs into the ear

the tongue loaded, unlicensed
and steaming with cordite
trying to finish something

nevah-shouda started

the tongue having kissed every wound from inside out
is jealous of bone

the tongue has heard of the heart
but doesn't believe in it
relies on the pulse in dice

the tongue as a wall, a bridge, a gate,
    fool's gold in moonlight

the tongue tied into a strait jacket, scatting

the tongue   a lead weight dropped
    onto a garden of peonies a nest of starlings

the tongue: misfired
        misplaced
        misspoke in our last conversation

the tongue   armed   blows a hole through its nearest cheek

the tongue thorny and uphill; single-bladed
and double-barreled

the tongue as museum, snowing through autumn

the tongue gets it   yes, yes, yes

but how it loves spitting No.

ULTRAVIOLET
Lake Merritt, Oakland

For Christian

My heart melts in your palm, Oakland—
Like a sun undressing itself in the bedroom of the ocean
The strobe lights pulsing along your horizon are mine
I blaze for you
                        Your cooling summer night swaddled in
cotton
If I give the season my all, pay me back
In a slot machine sky caching out stars

Since your streets never frost
Edit out my memories of snow and marbled dunes of salt
Your rich black earth free of plastic or any fakeness
Is the right soil to be transplanted

Sometimes I want everything darker
I wish even the daytime appreciated the elegance of black

Teach my skin your philosophy of breezes
Moving across me like a nor'easter having
Just learned to kiss

SOLITARY DAWN, QUARANTINE CITY
Various Boroughs

Walking predawn streets to a quarantined city—
its blocks antiseptically silent,
but there's still a trace of summer's blood in the gravel
and sheets of smoke drying in the overnight air.

To a rooster weeping in its sleep,
the dawn is bullshit
stubbornly proud of its poisoned colors.

The sun scissors at night's hem
        stars jiggle their baby teeth. My eyes
a delirious bride before the newness of the world.

In the prison of time, presence is freedom,
and memory will kick hope down a flight of stairs.
That god might be a junkie on the nod for human pain ain't lost on me,
not after misreading "Help Us" in a noose of rope-lights strangling a house.

The dawn's breath begins sketching ideas for the day.
You can hear dreamers solve equations in their sleep.
Phantom santas poxed in reds, whites wave drunkenly
from yards black as cemeteries.

                              The streets have ceased recycling—
                              they call for death or nothing.

MOMENT OF SILENCE
14th St., Oakland

a carrier cadillac on 22's
        lime green licked & left wet
                at the stop sign

flosses sparkling engagement rims of ice

the sun blushes orange
        over the street, observing
                the ship's captain

                his arms drip across the wheel
        beneath a wool lid
            rolled to military precision
                a stud of sweat sparkles at his jaw

the caddy purrs   before pouncing   on the twilight

U GET USED 2 THE CRAZIEST SHIT
Mandela Parkway, Oakland

last night impotent teens jacked semi-
automatic hard ons into virgin night thighs
freckled with stars

with each hot steel nut
flame busted
I call the name
of a lost love
or occupied grave
and tumble deeper asleep

I am not scared
I am not bothered
I am comforted

I accept the caged dog bark of drunk, angry
niggas like spontaneous prayers

I take the hot rubber bong hit of tires
dipping corners as speaking in tongues

I dance to the blues of police sirens

night weeping, to me, sounds like bird calls.

a rusted monte carlo turning a slow motion
donut on a screaming flat tire then chopping

down a stop light in the process isn't funny to me

how did I get used to such crazy shit?

at six in the morning   a butt naked crackhead
stomps up the street, screaming
I ain't nevah goin back   no mo…
to wherever it was she'd left—

her breasts loose as a blouse on a clothesline
—shag carpet, shag drapes—
three nomadic brothers seem to understand

they double park at lamp posts
then attempt to scoop her up from behind
in a jacket—imagine cape man
taking james brown off stage

but she wriggles loose   screams
waking strung out pigeons,
their feathers jheri-curled with fever.

three blocks later

it's still too early for the sun
when two women approach me, ask:

'Where are we? Where the fuck are we at?'

I don't know what to tell them—
earth? california? west oakland?

the girl speaks to the air between us—
we rode here with a nigga
last night
and he ditched us— They say
been walking blocks
all! night!

    I tell them:
you can follow me to the train station...
                      tumbled away in the
opposite direction

besides—who am I? what do I know?

that every crackhead starts out as a child.
bullets are sperm fertilizing eggs in reverse.
every heart beats for one wrong name.

NIGGA LOVER
Lakeshore Ave., Oakland

Sunday morning
and the only people
talking about love
are crazy.

This one woman
in a plastic bag tuxedo
& dirty sock tamale

stands in the doorway
of the coffeeshop,

*i'm not a nigga
i'm a nigga lover*

but no one hears her.

people pass
duck low

shielding their children
from the arterial spray
of her words

so crazy won't splash on them.
Still, she removes her shoes
& shouts into the mailbox,

i'm not a nigga
i'm a nigga lover!

Just then,
a white woman approaches
as if kindness
might be the cure.

She hands her a pastry
in a translucent bag

But she just turns
to her, eyes glistening
with the knowledge of
a thousand eclipsed moons
and says: *bitch*!

i'm not a nigga
i'm a nigga lover

and the white woman
smooths the wrinkles in her skirt
with her palms,
says,

well, I have to go now. you
take care.

and the woman in the sack
snatches up her shoes, her socks,
her recycle earth grocery purse

and marches away
from the coffee shop

words
spilling from her mouth
free and loose now
like tears at a funeral
over a person
having died
for nothing.

THE LAST TIME I PULLED OVER TO ASK FOR DIRECTIONS
Encinal Ave., Alameda, CA

We pull up
to a young brother with a storm-cloud afro
wearing a tank top

He stands at the entrance to a liquor store
over a cask barrel garbage can,
gutting a cigar of its black intestines.

Branches of a blunt licked flat in his fingers.

Y'all tryna get to High Street,
he says at us.

His eyebrows arch,
phototropic hair bubbles.

Across from him
a car full of shadows
idles, sleepily.

Y'all come thru the tunnel?
Yeah, we come thru the tunnel.

Right then, an old man approaches the store.
His hair a snow bank
Elbows a half foot behind him like handles

The young brother lollipop licks the cigar wrap:

Unc—you need a ride back?
We bout to roll out.

Yeah, Unc says,
And dissolves into the cool bath of the store.

Y'all need to go back to the tunnel,
he instructs.
And stay *allllllllllll* the way to your left…

There are a dozen l's trilling in his all.

It works: we can see it through his body,
a turf dancing bee freestyling directions.
From the smooth concrete entrance of the freeway

to the glowing letters reading
High Street,
predicting, in dual directions,
the same future
for us all.

WHEN THEY ROLLBACK PRICES ON YO MAMA'S SODA
Peralta and 14th St., Oakland

Hey man,
hey.

A middle aged man waddles off the sidewalk
in front of the corner grocery store.
The street is Sunday-afternoon empty
except for a Cadillac idling at the light.

Hey man— hey!
His face grimaced and gray.

He hangs his weight
on the driver's side door

then says to the man inside:

Let me borrow a dolla.
I gotta get my momma a can of soda.

The car answers by pulling away.

The man appears stranded.
As I pass, he looks over at me:

Man, please
a dolla—

my momma

—he says.

I tell him I'm out

& gradually
his momma's can of soda
gets marked down.

But my pockets are more empty than his.

A second man appears to guard the grocery store entrance.

A kind of Steppin Cerberus, he is spindly & gaunt & old.
His eyes are the color of brake lights.
He pushes himself off the door frame as I stroll by.

Do you have
35 cents
?

Words, cumbersome in his mouth.
He wobbles backwards as in a trust fall
& is caught by the building

nearly missing my disembodied
no.

I'm walking these streets
freshly high

myself

but I can still
see
what's
really going on.

SANDWICH SCHOOL
Telegraph Ave., Oakland

Gimme a turkey sandwich with everything, no onions.
I don't want them things. What's that?
Red bell pepper taste like water. Nasty!
And pickles! I want pickles. Extra pickles.

I don't want them things. What's that?
Olives is nasty. Yellow cheese! The yellow kind.
What kind of bread is that? Brown? Ugh.
Did y'all put honey mustard? I'm watching y'all.

Olives is nasty. Yellow cheese! The yellow kind.
What kind of bread is that? Brown? Ugh.
Did y'all put honey mustard? I'm watching y'all.
Look— ain't you been to sandwich school? Damn.

What kind of bread is that? Brown? Ugh.
That's too much lettuce. That don't look right.
Ain't you been to sandwich school? Damn.
I'm allergic to tomatoes. Just—Oh, hell naw.

That's too much lettuce. That don't look right.
Red bell pepper tastes like water. Nasty!
I'm allergic to tomatoes. Just—Oh, hell naw.
Gimme a turkey sandwich with everything, no onions.

OVERHEARD IN DR TIM'S OFFICE
College Ave., at Broadway, Oakland

where
was that
pizza place
we saw

what was it

a dolla
seventy five
a slice

two dollaz

I'm hungry
as a grave

I was up
with the rain
last night

sitting
on the front
porch

smoking

tryna cry

WHERE U TRY'N 2 GO?
43rd St., Oakland

I get up to go to the bathroom.

At the front door of the house
there is no doorknob:

*Now, see that hunk of metal
above you,* he said.

There was a quarter-sized
curtain mount nailed
near the top of the door.

*Push that back
& pull the door towards you.*

I pinch the metal lip
push it, then stick
my other finger
in the hole
where a door handle
once was.

The door opened
onto a heavily draped
dark porch.

Now for the door out there,

he said. *Up at the top,
there's a latch with a hook
on it. Just pull that.*

Then:

*Now here's what you do
to get back in.*

*Knock on the window
three times
& do the hokey pokey,* he coughs.

I walk down the front steps
pull out the garbage can
jammed between
the edge of the house
& a red Chevy
on blocks.

Then up the driveway
until I get to the boat
on a trailer.

Stand there in the dark
while voices from inside
circle me like laughing moths

& release what remained
of the beers & Patron
shots into the mud.

Then, retracing my steps
down the driveway,
I push the garbage can
back in place,
climb the front porch,
& knock on the window three
times
until footfalls bang
on the hardwood floor inside.

A woman's voice
announces: *This is the ghetto. Shit.*
& laughs.

GOLD FLIP FLOPS & SUNFLOWER SEEDS
East 24th and 9th Ave., Oakland

siren stands sentry on an empty street corner feet aflame in gold flip flops
I got to give her half my check / you got to have money to be broke
barking directions into a .38 caliber cell phone like she held hostages
I gotta have some place to go / based off this right here right here

I got to give her half my check / you got to have money to be broke
Are you planning to disappear? I hope to leave my family &
disappear wit you
I gotta have some place to go / based off this right here right here
beneath a sky peaching feathery reds, blue cheese clouds

Are you planning to disappear? I hope to leave my family &
disappear wit you
barking directions into a .38 caliber cell phone like she held hostages
beneath a sky peaching feathery reds, blue cheese clouds
siren stands sentry on an empty street corner feet aflame in gold flip flops

TINA TURNER'S WIG GIVES ITS FINAL PUBLIC ADDRESS
Charm Beauty College, Grand Ave., Oakland

I ain't no wig. I am a high jeweled crown
heliotrope to the spotlight.
I may not have roots but anyone can see
we– all of us– are inseparable
The first compassionate partner she ever got to choose

She sat me on her knee–not like a doll,
but a sister–and chanted herself empty.

The care she needed
she massaged into each lock
She said: You better be good to me
said her real name was Anna Mae
then told every pebble of her story
between Nutbush to Buckingham Palace

She explained I was her new legacy–shiny and divine
handcrafted, purified in ceremony, then left to dry natural

I was sewed and ruffled
back combed and teased
until I could defy gravity.

And how high I could rise for her
It's because of me fans recognize her
before she ever opens her mouth.

Everyone goes on about her insured legs,
the girls she calls them.
I've heard of them.

But I am her marquee
I shine like the rainbow of light
god sent before swearing off more rain.

Oh my lady
How long I'd been meaning to tell you
Every strand every fiber
Every thing depends on love

BEAUTICIAN'S SON
Market St., Oakland

af
ro'd
muscle
boy pumps
cinder   block   iron
out back. shoulders, chest swell
to a new tire's firmness. kitchen
falls quiet
nearest the
w i n d o w .
hair cools at
the stove

CLOTHESLINE
Market St., Oakland

I.

Our lives transmitted through the clothesline

its pulley and wire clove hitched
through an oxide-red steel turnbuckle
bolted to the back porch

Our molted, spectral epidermis:

my mother's Dacron beautician's smock / its winged coachman's collar

my father's blue green boiler suit / shirts rinsed of their catfish
sweat and Reno aftershave

        church shirts and blue skirts
        twirl and twerk fast and loose;

blouses badged with bird droppings and butterflies

hand washed lace, silk chemise slips, elephant skinned long johns,
cable knitted turtlenecks

flash dried above applauding fruit trees and tiny impact craters
pocketing water

II.

A line of laundry flat ironed beneath an unexpected tempest from a
black rope of clouds

A storm of salt shaken from the sky.

      Sometimes, the weather makes the clothesline a burden.

Its green cable becomes a rest stop for dripping robins and blue jays.

Duvets, upper sheets and quilts
would need to be carried down to the laundromat anyway.

I, too, have ruined one wash load or many

after destroying handmade cities of topsoil
by plowing up fistfuls of sand atomized to dust.

All for the joy of smoke and pelting debris
after television's prettiest explosions

then drying my grimy hands
on the pink towels surrendering above.

III.

Our washing machine's summer diet
of salty, sweat enhanced t-shirts and hot pants
from a carload of cousins,

flaked with corn chips

perfumed in exhaust, sugar, and cheese.

Forgiven into cleanliness
beneath a flagellating sun.

Our skin mingled with every element.

The biometric intelligence of thread and yarn
infused with skin cells

the whispers of a sun crisped towel
licking beads of shower water from your thighs

the healing curtain of the clothesline

its metallic song pulled for decades into extinction.

WHAT ZERO SOUNDS LIKE (AFTER WATCHING TEENAGERS ATTEMPT TO USE A ROTARY PHONE)
Market St., Oakland

There used to be one in every house
affixed to the kitchen wall or
on its own end table or altar.

Our bone white phone
ruled from a wire stand crammed
with phone books and
addresses torn from envelopes.
If you remembered to clean it
you'd wipe it down like a baby–
its umbilical cord would braid itself
over all the stories and lies transmitted.
You'd have to stand on a dining room chair
to let the long cord unkink

the handset   a satellite
spinning weightless
above the rug.

You *slow dialed*
if you didn't want to talk
but had to. You'd
listen to its metallic purr,
watch the plastic wheel rotate
and as it rang

wondered what
    the house
        or room
            on the other end
looked like. Ours would scream
in our empty living room
and you'd run to it.
Tell it from the kitchen
you were coming,
even as every footfall
shook the decorative plates
on the walls.

        Sometimes,
momma could tell who was on the line
just by hearing it ring.
She'd say: *Jesus!*
before picking it up—
not because it was Him calling—
but rather she knew she was going to need Him
before she hung up.

Grandpa would call every day
and hold the phone.
You'd stand there and listen to him
breathe for a while.
You had to wait—even if you knew what he wanted
And what he wanted was

        nothing. Just nothing.

Where yo momma, he'd finally say
his mouth echoing toothless m's.
Momma would lean back on the couch,
his voice in her ear,
and they'd exchange breaths for the longest time.
She'd sit like that for a while
smoking, her fingers turning
solitaire tarot on the coffee table.

Sometimes she'd lean back on the couch
and I'd put my ear to her stomach
listening to what was going on in there
      until she had to Get Up
           and Do This or Finish That.

Call waiting used to be called Patience.
You let the phone ring and if no one picked up
you called right back, let it ring some more.

Call forwarding was when someone would call
and it wasn't for you.
You'd have to go to the yard
where she spray-watered tomato plants
or you'd hang out the window above the driveway
or shout through the bathroom door: *Phone!*

It's true there was a number to call just to hear the time.
Actually, it wasn't a number at all: you dialed *Popcorn.*

There was a number to dial for movie times
There was a number to dial for dirty whispers

There was a number to dial to hear a psychic
        tell you everything you didn't know about your own life
There was a number to dial to hear a joke
The joke was that call cost ten dollars and there
was no number to dial to get your money back.

There was a number to dial to save money on a long distance call
You had to dial another number before dialing the number you
wanted to dial

Long distance only happened Sunday nights–
You sat with your parents and shouted
over the width of states.
The caller's voice so far away they sounded other worldly.
You had to talk quick and with purpose–
remember your report card and ask about your cousin–
because time was money tumbling from someone's palm.

As a teen, I could talk for hours about Nothing.
Or prank call. I talked with a girl once
while slowly pouring water
out of a gallon pitcher into the toilet.
It took the longest time before she asked:
What are you doing?!?
Oh, just standing here, I said.

Obscene calls don't happen anymore.
I miss them.
One day
my father caught one
and said: *Hold on for a minute*

then passed the phone
to Uncle Jerry, who'd just drove 270 miles
from Bakersfield.

He took the phone, listened
for a good while, frowned, then
started cussing till black flies tumbled from his mouth.
That was back when hanging up on someone really meant
something.

THREE VARIATIONS
Palo Alto, CA / Stamford, TX / Los Angeles, CA

*)	that house, nested amongst drowsy trees, its patio and garden delirious with rain. The walls are lined with photographs like tree rings tracing a confirmed lineage. I watch her father, standing above a table-scape of blue cupcakes, his belly a perfect teardrop of meat. What life flashed before his eyes then, staring at bowls of smoked salmon and girders of green beans while two senile dogs, both shivering and blind, made endless circles at his feet? Past the appetite's horizon, what within him still hungered?
*)	that house, its walls black as oxidized blood. Hanging on the living room wall, a lenticular print of Jesus regaining consciousness on the cross. Seen from different angles, He blinks as if, with hands and feet nailed, something fell into his eye: crumb of pollen, eyelash, splinter. The house around it, a black hole swallowing emotion. Our eldest aunt, without children or a living husband, trembles beneath a shroud of ghosts. She rages in praise of the darkness and her concussed Jesus bleeding light. I watch my father in his cowboy hat. What life flashed before him then? A galaxy of choices made and declined. While my aunt raged against the machinery of her own mind, I stood across from him in the kitchen, a stranger's boy. What kind of man would he have been for his real son, forged by whiskey and a stack of blues 45s, yet abandoned quick as a half-smoked Marlboro from a Buick window? What shifted within him as he looked at me and lowered his gaze?
*)	that house, roaches commuting its expressway of walls; mounds of sour laundry sprouting philodendrons and spider plants. My cousin stands in the living room, holding his pillow-sized daughter midair while she convulses and shivers, a trick neither he

nor her body understood. His wife tosses the warm doll of their son onto my lap and stands, as you might for royalty. Around us, everything fell away into a white noise of sloppy prayers, except the words: *Jesus, Telephone, Hospital.* Sometimes prayers fall in a monsoon of iron. He said: She was lying on my chest, tracing my fingernails... And now, all vibration and static. What life flashed before him then? What kind of life leaves one carrying the debt of mercy?

BENJAMIN'S WITNESSES
6300 Mission St., Daly City

Time doesn't weep over extinct sales jobs.
Remember *The Watkins Lady?* Her

bottomless basket of spices, extracts,
salves and lotions, stories and debts

Feet pounded into paws over decades of miles across city borders;
market adeline san pablo grove—20 blocks west, 30 blocks east.

She was thought to be rich despite her sun-jerky cheeks,
a professional bag lady OK being tipped: *Not Today Maybe Next Time.*

She might've laughed in my face to learn there was only one job
I applied for and quit the same day. I didn't know I couldn't do it.

That morning I sat *not eating* in McDonalds
amongst cohorts in Goodwill suits and Salvation Army ties

when I could only afford to be hungry in flea market couture.
I spent my first workday shadowing a Mexican youngster

through our randomly selected neighborhood. We resembled
unlicensed detectives or witnesses for bragged-over Benjamin's never held.

I don't remember what we sold / Pretty Nothing / Snake-Free Snake Oil
But he was omni-competent / A master salesperson /All heart and
mouthpiece

But until we arrived at our first house, I never noticed
the thick keloid smirking across his throat, ear to ear.

It was the color of an earthworm, segmented and long.
One lonely grandmother let us in. Her crisp living room

with its faculty board of children
in a pyramid of photos on the wall.

My coworker stood and set off a fountain
of promises with the confidence of a prophet.

The woman and I sat in wonder over the committed
silence of his wound. We awaited his story of resurrection

and the bill we'd have to pay to hear it. The truth was
he and I sold no liniment, no cinnamon,

no bottled Christ or cleanser. Us pitiful boys.
Useless to mommas and grandmommas

on every block, in every zip code. The Watkins lady
seemed to have what everybody needed. We just needed to live.

PREFACE TO A PHOTOGRAPH: 1976
11th Ave., Delano Ca.

three black men
spooned from the same bowl
stand embracing in my father's mobile home

the lightning flash of them frozen
in the amber of 1976

their rhyming eyes
sparkle like lit matches

men don't smile, but they are happy.
arms interlocked long as the interstate

it is night

in every room where my father stands,
there is a river

here a hot river
        sweetened with perch
laps the drawn curtain

three black men

        blues singers of borderless ache

        soldiers

  gamblers
  cowboys

the mahogany concentration
of my father's 10,000-mile highway stare

Cousin J.D. in a 1970's plaid juicy fruit leisure suit

And their great uncle Iley
  a human spear in a tweed flat cap
    chin up and flaring like a knife

WORM'S EASTER SUNDAY MONOLOGUE
Bakery Concession Window, Market St., San Francisco, CA

I woke up Sunday, right? Cuz
I ain't even knowed
it was Easter: I'm on the phone like, Huh
and my cousin was on the phone saying—
Can Junior come with us to hunt Easter eggs.
And I'm like: Why.

Cause its Easter, Nigga.
When.
Today. Right now.
I was like—Shit, I don't care.

I ain't religious. I didn't know it was Easter
cause I don't go to church.

I don't even know what that's all about.

So I got up
and sent my son off to do Easter egg hunting
and I was like—house to myself. Beautiful, right?
The day was cracking though.
I figure since its Easter I'd go ahead
and do my part, *naw-mean*?
I went in the backyard right
and raked up a lot of them leaves and shit...
All them storms we had an everything—
I ain't had the chance to get out there, *knowwhatimsayin*.

An den

I cleaned up the grill, got that smoking.
Smoked out the whole neighborhood—Smoked em out.
Made some chicken and some spare ribs. Oh hell yeah.
That shits nice. I got some skills. I'll put you out of business.

EASTER WEEKEND, MIAMI
Collins Ave., at 14th St

Round midnight, the drunk dentist at the bar
says, "I don't want to see another tooth
before Monday. Fuck every abscess."
So I clamp my mouth shut
as I would to the abstract syllables
of a foreign language.
Once he learns I'm from California,
he high-fives me, despite at that very moment
my entire state was slobbering rain.

While awaiting food, he hands me his phone.
In the 90's this would have been a brochure.
On it, another man speaks of the thieves
displayed on crosses next to Jesus;
Ordained, forgiven and first to be polished in the blood.

And right then a young woman walks by
or maybe she's a girl in her sister's dress
who notably does not smile
when the dentist disrupts her, motions to me, says:
Here he is, honey. The man you're out here looking for.

FLIRTING PHLEBOTOMISTS
Summit St. Pill Hill Oakland, CA

she straps me to a high chair like it's my last night a bachelor
once i peel out of my shirt, shit gets real

    I might have to turn the fan on, she says

She flips her cherry box braids like a cat o' nine tails

After tying me off, she smacks my arm for the first juicy bulge
but my hide-and-seek veins get blood shy
        reverse flow
                capillaries shrink
                        baby lick the needles tip
   so she calls for backup

I was just getting some, she said. *Then it stalled and stopped.*

Girl, tell me about it

The second tech had old tricks, of course
        her fingers dowsing, tapping code on my arm like checking
a melon for sugar

He offered his neck a minute ago, the first tech said
He wanted to neck? the second one gasped
That's what he say, the first insisted,
        With both arms petted and frisked, I blushed a new color
Ooh, but that second tech knows the call and response of blood

how every blessed cell surged towards her like a hungry school of fish

MARQUIS
Steuart St., San Francisco

i guess i have a mulatto
grandson now

he was born
yesterday
at 3 o'clock

you know, that hospital
is the same one
where my daughter was born
almost
   ... 20 years ago?

       his dad
is in that
facility
down there

in Vacaville.

Do you
      know it?

I think the judge

or somebody

felt sympathy
for him

cause he's a good kid...

just got in a little trouble
for fighting.

& sent the guy to the hospital.

      it's a shame
he missed the birth.

won't get out
before
thanks
   giving.

marquis.

she named him... marquis.

ever heard anybody
with that name?

is it
common?

I looked it up.

marquis de sade

where we get the word

sadism.

    Did you know that?

PAYCHECKS AND BALANCES
Embarcadero Plaza, San Francisco, CA

One year, I was dropped into the financial district
like a battered filet dunked in cold grease

The job I thought I wanted:
        purchaser at a condom warehouse in San Francisc

The job I got:
        managing office supplies for a law firm

First day on the job, my boss—
        the only black woman in the office,
took me to lunch

So terrified I might be asked
to pay for the salad I ordered,
I began counting leaves for a possible lay-away plan

She was forthright   humorless
sitting across from me erect as a buzzard

and here lies my dying heart, open and aromatic

She said: I am a tough person to work for

She was

It was the last peaceful conversation we'd have

I would complete each task to the letter, yet she remained displeased

changing her goals and urgency, mid-action

She'd march down to my dungeon
and scan the supply room for mistakes, oversight, neglect

Her assistant shivering behind her, transcribing

Every night I'd return to my small room in the Mission
and weep into my bank account

If she'd ask me to rappel down the building and scrub the windows
I'd have to do it

just for her to circle every spot I missed

I was paid to be destroyed

I couldn't quit   I couldn't afford hate
So I took it   by the forkful   for three weeks

Then one day, she called out sick

      and never returned to the office

After a while, I was afraid to ask

Her absence went unremarked, building-wide,
as if it was a kind of superstition

On our five floors
I was the only black person left
and I had it easy

The only one to ever see me and speak the truth

was gone

DAVE'S WEDDING
West St., Oakland

This was the first wedding I ever attended. My friend Dave became re-acquainted with the best friend of his former girlfriend. (His ex remarried 10 years previously.) He and this best friend have been talking for three weeks. After I'd been playing phone tag with him for several days, he called back and said: "We're getting married." I broke out laughing. After catching my breath, he said: "We're getting married Friday. And I need you to be the best man."

Friday night, after leap frogging interviews at temp agencies in San Francisco, I arrived in Oakland stressed and broke and scared to leave the station until I knew for certain he was home. He had several errands to run and I was paranoid he'd be running late, but he wasn't. He had just gotten out of the bathtub when I arrived at his apartment, standing in a robe that made him look like Isaac Hayes on the cover of *Black Moses*. John Singleton's *Baby Boy* was on TV, the scene where a naked Ving Rhames awkwardly meets his new girlfriend's adult son. Dave explained how much he felt like Rhames's unwelcome character in that film, since his fiancée's two youngest children had some issues over the whole marriage thing. One threatened to move out, the other was tripping, Dave explained. Her oldest, the 18-year-old, announced, "Y'all ain't getting no younger," and left it at that.

So Dave stood shrugging before his closet. He handed me the $20 he'd promised when we talked over the phone. Then, nodded me over to his kitchen. He seasoned chicken wings but didn't have time to cook them. He handed me a container of still-marinating chicken then said, *Let's go do this.*

We picked up his fiancée, movie-star pretty in a simple, warm dress. Dave told me she is studying to be a minister and we were driving to meet her mentor. The three of us were quiet, me in the backseat of the truck, cradling a sealed bowl of chicken wings. Every block or two she would glance over at him. I tossed a couple of jokes to shatter the dense silence, but mostly we drove with the radio whispering jazz.

Her mentor's church was a converted garage beneath a large Victorian in West Oakland. Thirty or forty folding chairs, a red rug, a drum set. The pastor was a middle-aged woman with cocoa butter skin and thick braids crowning her shoulders like an Egyptian headdress. The bride handed me a disposable camera and the four of us prayed. The pastor spoke briefly about the lifelong responsibilities of couples. She was articulate and wise. Then she said, "We are gathered here today..." When she got to the line, "If there are any present here today who have just cause why this man and this woman should not be united, let him speak now or forever hold his peace," she looked up at me. I said: "I'm cool."

The newlyweds kissed. I snapped photos. I signed witness documents. Dave gave the pastor a "love offering," a sealed envelope that she slid into her jacket pocket. The three of us returned to the truck in a gentle rain. The bride said rain was a good luck blessing on newlyweds. I'd forgotten the tradition about rice.

They dropped me off at the train station. Mr. and Mrs., just like that. As the truck pulled away, I thought, "Where are the cans? There should be cans and noise, right? And *Just Married* scrawled in soap on the truck's gate." But there was just me standing on the corner holding a cold container of marinating chicken wings in the rain.

THE FLORIST
West MacArthur and 40th, Oakland

after smoking
whatever it was
down to its last flake
of ash

he comes into the flower shop
approaches the florist and says:

what flower
cuts through the bullshit
between people

and says:
I don't hate you
despite never saying I love you

that apologizes
without being
sorry

that
means love
without saying it

and says love
without
meaning death

and the florist says:
the yellow chrysanthemum

BONFARE: FINE FOOD FAST
East 30th St., Oakland

It was the only store in my new neighborhood I hadn't visited.
I was attracted to it because it was bigger and brighter than my corner liquor store–
the one where the man behind the counter danced and sang for Allah because I didn't buy alcohol on New Year's Eve.

I walked three extra blocks to investigate the store but the place looked empty with its drive thru aisles. There were more shelves than things displayed.

Five loaves of white bread, bottles of motor oil, hamburger buns bleached to an impure whiteness. A golden retriever appeared to jump off a bag of food.

At least they had bananas.

Pears, apples, shelves full of wine bottles,

glass refrigerators bloated with beer and ice frame the store.

I found cooking oil and leaned in to make certain the medium-sized bottle was
stamped 6.75.

The olive oil was over 10.

I bought a small bottle, grabbed a bag of chips, bottle of juice then

stood behind
a woman in radioactive pink, her shoulders an expanse of moles like beached starfish.

I noted the man behind the counter, the sheer cliff of his mustache.

His eyes found me and registered disgust.

He rings up 7.81. I have 6, sigh and hand him the 20 I didn't want to break.

He plops two dimes into my palm and a matching two dollars.

Didn't I hand you a twenty, I say.

And he says: Oh yeah, then, bingo slaps a 10 in my hand like I'd just won it.

THE ONLY CHILD
43rd and Market, Oakland

Silent, single resident of the bombed out living room.
Tiny thug scout in track braids and jeans
already dripping past hips no wider than a squash.
The three-year-old sits in one of the deep craters
on the couch, folding into his psp console as if learning to pray.

He hovers beneath the radar of his father's story
of the repo men who tried to reclaim his Escalade.
Next to his father sits a woman cruising men on BlackSingles.com
who claim to live in Folsom without state-issue chains around their
necks.

His father slams Patron shots and loudly rakes weed into pyramids
on record sleeves.

Suddenly, the boy rolls off the sofa, urgently waving the game,
and approaches his father.

The man pauses his story of repo men and his M-14 kept propped
at the front door like a broom, then diagnoses:
Boy! You ain't got enough money to buy no guns!

He takes the game under thick, affectionate thumbs, his forearm
enclosing the boy who squeezes onto his father's lap staring
bright-eyed at the glowing device.

He laughs.

Between square tablets of his teeth comes a sound shattering the
room's low gray fog
causing the rest of us drunks to fall away from father and son like so
many empty shells.

MAN-TALK

Buriel Clay Memorial Theater, San Francisco

> *Of the 99 Names of Allah, #35 Ash-Shakur = The Rewarder of Thankfulness*

Ash-Shakur, the five-year-old afro,
leads me by hand to the barren stage.
The auditorium is empty except for us.

He paces the stagewidth
leaving me to critique his solo
from the front row.
He heckles himself with requests: *Hey!*
He says: *Wanna see me do a flip?*

I say: Don't break your neck.

With less than a bird's effort
he climbs mid-air and spins
a sparkler of naps and limbs
landing softly on both feet.

Hey! He says. *Wanna see me do the splits?*

Sure, man.

He slides down into a perfect
Jean-Claude Van Damme.

I think,

turkey wishbone at thanksgiving
when I say aloud:

Make a wish.

And he looks into my sarcastic mouth, says:

I wish you were my dad.

*

The parking lot behind the theater.

A single shopping cart, no cars.

I push him fast,
        faster,
until his hair sweeps back,
he laughs–fully automatic,
long clip of teeth.

Once I've run myself out,
we sit by the stage door–
two guys at the end of a day's work.

He leads the conversation.
Inventories
his life, his friends
as if we were catching up
over the years spilled between us.

He talks about his step-mom
        whom I just met
prepping in the dressing room for rehearsal

He talks about his mom,

        then his forgetful dad
who once forgot to shut his bedroom door:

…that thing,
Ash Shakur says mid-story.

*That thing you use
to have sex with?*

A… Condom…? I say

Yeah… *Yeah!!*

And it's here
where his step-mom
gently leans into our conversation
from the doorway behind us:

        *What
are you talking about?*

Ash Shakur: *It's just man stuff.*

Step-Momma: *Y'all need to talk about something else.*

Then she looks at me,
the bad uncle,
bearing the weight
of all fault.

Ash-Shakur

and I sit,
say nothing else.

Later that night
as the lights come up
a voice is thrown
towards me from the audience in the dark:
That's my friend up there.

Then: *Shhhhh…*

SCARS
#40 Bus North Bound, Telegraph Ave., Berkeley

The scar is delicate and coarse, yawning teeth like a zipper. My cousin raises his curtain-red shirt and we stare at his horrible trophy, a thick black eel tapering off at the center of his chest. He invites us to touch it, but none do. "But this new bitch right here," he says. Lifting his pant leg, he shows us a clunky gray bracelet on his ankle, big as a museum-age cell phone. He fingers it, scratching hard.

a) You either make your struggles your strength or your excuse
b) I am a number right now. I'm not a man, not a father, I am a number
c) Scars appear as pie crust to my tongue. I feel uncomfortable saying that among strangers
d) He was once considered a miracle child
e) Other. Please Explain: _____

GHOST HOMIES
San Leandro Blvd., San Leandro

Don't feel bad about yourself, but you a lunatic. First time I see that? I'm out.
Go on with your afterlife… You just wanna be a ghost the whole time? Punkass.
I ain't gon lie. You did your thing. You came from the other side and actually grabbed me.
You can have all this of what you got– I'mma get up outta here.

Go on with your afterlife… You just wanna be a ghost the whole time? Punkass.
That sucks. You got a child sitting there ripe for possession.
You can have all this of what you got– I'mma get up outta here.
Ghost tryin' to put hands on people. I ain't here for that. Squad out! We gotta go, G! Burn. It. Down.

That sucks. You got a child sitting there ripe for possession.
I ain't gon lie. You did your thing. You came from the other side and actually grabbed me.
Ghost tryin' to put hands on people. I ain't here for that. Squad out! We gotta go, G! Burn. It. Down.
Don't feel bad about yourself, but you a lunatic. First time I see that? I'm out.

NOBODY WANTS TO HEAR WHAT GOD HAS TO SAY ABOUT LOVE
Outer Sunset, San Francisco

I lost my notebook talking shit—
Blame the ventriloquism of tequila!

The bottle lost its virginity
to my clumsy fingers
and a right-handed knife used left-handed

causing folks to run screaming from the kitchen.

But then it was glass after glass—
more fire than water—especially the rounds I made.

The worm was pupating in my subconscious, ya'll.

I was puppet to circumstance
my hands poltergeists tripping on gin.

And there were more shots to be had
when we crawled to the bar
sending my memory into oblivion
and hot Filipina women to shout rainbows into the street.

I thought my notebook fell out of my back pocket
while in the backseat of her car.

I was with the Homie and his girlfriend—

whom I still barely know—at the end of the night,
'bout to pull out of the parking space.

When Out Of Nowhere
my Baptist preacher grandfather
came back down to earth
to tell these young people about love.

Through me! Hail Glory!
And I began speaking in tongues
like the old days, snake-throwing days

Preaching about Love
The promise of love! The miracle of love!
The future of love!
How love was brought down from the mountaintop.
God said: Let it rain on 'em!

And just when I found my rhythm
and brought out the white handkerchief,
the Homie as deacon and congregation both
turns to me from the passenger seat, says:

Would you shut the fuck up?!?

But I can't!
Having been moved by the spirits,
wave upon wave of love-knowledge crashes
until he raises his hand
like a witness to sin and says:

You wanna take this shit outside?

I'm already outside, nigga!
Someone said bring it! so here it is!

Night comes alive around me like never before.

I'm first in the ring
        and first on the ground.

I look up: heaven glows in a license plate

and God drops the beat for
I Ain't No Joke on my forehead.
Until the Homie's girlfriend appears in a vision
at the back of the car, arms folded in angels' wings
and says:

If you boys don't get in this car RIGHT NOW
And Shut the Hell Up
I'mma leave ya'll drunk asses here in the street.

Where did that come from?
She was such a nice girl before.

With hydraulic blackness, the Homie
claps me off the ground.

and it was HERE where my notebook fell out of my pocket

…which was probably for the best…

For the rest of the ride home
I quietly gave myself a backseat exorcism.
Grandpa gave a quick benediction, packed up his revue
and moved out of my chest.

Ain't nobody trying to hear about love right now…

BUS TRANSFER
#57 West Bound, Oakland

an old white dude,
his gray hair cornrowed & tinted blue,
runs for the oncoming bus.

he drags behind him
a fat chihuahua on a leash,
a yellow grub blinded by an oversized raincoat.

the bus roars to the stop, rain sizzles on the asphalt.

the man jumps onto the bus
through the rear exit door
        with the chihuahua
still being dragged behind him.

the dog's head
bangs against
the bottom stair
of the bus
with a bassy
THUMP.

Come on,
the old man
says.

THE BOY IN THE ROTC UNIFORM
580 FWY near Fruitvale

        resembles a general in miniature
Fully uniformed, he is chubby
but solid as a truck.

When the light changes
I watch him cross the intersection
before an idle of cars at the freeway exit.

As he walked, some unseen thing
within him appeared to kick.

He stopped at the corner from where
I was standing at the bus stop
and began aggressively digging in his pocket
for a white inhaler.

He screams for breath through it
bending like a saxophone player

before producing a bright white bulb
from his throat. He braces himself against

a light pole, then stands
still as if he'd fallen asleep on his feet.

Before I make any decision
a bus

like an inverted moon
rises over the butte across the street.

The boy approaches
and jumps behind me
until I turn to tell him,
it's not my bus, youngster.

*

The sun climbs.
Night thaws.
Bleary headlights rush the freeway into rapids.

I wait.

There was this one time
when I
found my cousin Isaac
brought to his knees
on our back porch.

Not quite
a full hour had passed
after checking him out of Merritt.

Finished he was
with hospitals,
marriages and
everything else.

At first
I thought he was praying

but with his whole body

as if in a hurry to expel everything
within him
he could not explain
to god.

DONATE TO THE CRAZY FUND
Tenderloin, San Francisco

Donate to the crazy fund,
he said.
He was an older man
festooned in white hair
standing on the corner
in a black and gold sorcerer's
cap, the tension in his hands
crushing his empty paper
cup.

One dollar
from my pocket
appears in my palm
in compulsive magic.

I tip him for nothing.

Yet, as I stand there
he says:
> You know,
> It costs twenty-eight dollars
> a night
> for a bed
> at that damn shelter
> And I was held down
> and raped
> by four animals

February 4.

*And the staff down there
did nothing about it!
They don't care, man.
Can you believe that?*

What I believe
is 27 more dollars
probably won't help.

He turns to one of the women
who stroll up behind me.

Donate to the crazy fund,
he says.

And the young brunette laughs
—which is all either of them gave.

Finally, the light I was waiting for
turns green.

I just stand there.

Where was I going?

A BLUES FROM THE BOOK OF BOB
Elder Care Facility, San Pablo., CA

1. Standing at the foot of the evangelist's bed, I glance shyly over the oceanic patience of her sleeping face.
2. I look around. What else is there to do here but sleep?
3. Not since those evenings with my mother, grandfather, and aunt have I stood in a place *this* void of expectation.
4. I turn from *staring* at Mother Sims' face
5. to study the pulsing ember of a television *angled* on a dresser in a room across the hall.
6. The arctic blue box provides the room's *only* color and conversation.

7. Some people won't visit places like this;
8. Its smell of antiseptic death panhandling at the building's dusty sidewalks.

9. Minutes cascade down my desire to leave.

10. Once I turn towards the light of the exit, she stirs.

11. The sheet breaks beneath her chin. A thin hand scratches her nose. Stars glitter beneath long black lashes as her eyes dawn to the room.

12. She compels me to *sit* along sheets white-capping the shoreline of her bed.

13. We hold hands.

14. Several years before, Mother Sims drew a cross in prayer oil on my mother's souring forehead and called in favors from Jesus who, at that time, would not take any.

16. Mother Sims says: I'm ninety-five now.
17. She is more lucid and regal and alive than some *men* a quarter her age.
18. She anoints herself my *godmother*, chanting my lineage, an epic poem of names, a combination to a lock.

19. At one point, in one of her memories, she says *something* that makes me, in *this* place, laugh.
20. The *woman* in the next bed–stirred by my outburst–snatches up the room divider as if skirt-checking virgins in Catholic school dorms.
21. She stares at me.
22. It is a gaze so desperate, I fail to return it.

23. The woman drops the panel, then begins to moan a bluesy dirge for someone named Bob.

24. Bob!!!
25. His name, a death rattle in her throat.
26. *Bob!!! Quit standing out there in the hallway drinking and cussing and carrying on.*
27. Bob, what's wrong? Come on home. *All is forgiven…*

28. Your dinner sits *here,* fresh and warm, with us! Take your seat at the head of the table, Bob. I've been cooking all night and ironing place settings since dawn.
29. Sweat is my cooking grease. These doilies are still wet from this morning's blood. Everything done has been done for *you.*

30. *Bob,* she says. *Come on in from the hallway. Bob? Bob!!*

31. Oh, shut up. Shut her up! Mother Sims says.
32. She closes her eyes and sneers in disgust at even the curtain separating them.
33. Mother Sims reaches over, grips my arm tight. *Tighter*!

34. As if to keep me from falling into whatever pit her mind so frantically lathers.

A FAMILY DINNER IN BERKELEY
University and Shattuck, Berkeley

macrame mom
in a raccoon hip bone
necklace,
permanent
near-sighted squint,
& a thousand years
of breasts growing
out of her stomach,
sits at the head
of the table
laundering napkins
in a water glass
she mops brown rice with her fork,
eats chopped
peanut gristle
fingertips at a time

the dad chews
for conversation
his temples boiling
skin & veins
hair at his crown
thinned to wisps
of fog. his gray
forearm a blurred
gate locked
before his place

the oldest son,
tie-dyed
jingling red dwarf
dog tags— cable
thick ropes of hair
down the length
of his back,
his chin a feral
riverbank
of razor grass

the youngest son's
pyrotechnic hair
spirals outward
into abstract
thought balloons

mom rolls the wet
dough of napkins
between her fingers
& laughs towards her sons

her eyes
submerged
behind a moonrise
of glasses

the eldest boy
recites the absurd epic poem
of their dietary restrictions:

no complex carbs, no milk,
no noodles, no butter
no tofu, no gluten, no sugar
no nothing   nothing and nothing again

all our guts, the boy says
                              are just…

he leaves no word there

his lips burst open
splattering sound

father eats.
mother forges totems
of wet napkins
the youngest boy,
his rice in ruins
monologues from boundless
bronze eyes

no one listens

IDEAS OF HOME
Market St., Oakland

climate of ice-blue smoke in the living room

our hound dog, hearing thunder as a riot of hooves
—begs peace from our simmering fish tank

      amethyst-eyed peas
mixing bowls of copper pennies whipped into dollars at Christmas

salon-pink styling rollers = circus peanuts with a hanger
deep fried transmission plugs on wax paper at the church bake sale

pubescent plum and nectarine trees anointed after nights' sermon
congregation of turnips giggle & gossip

philodendrons drop green climbing ropes
to sip pot-liquor off greens

home brewed holy water
consecrated toast weeps miracle rings of butter

auto repair manuals like greasy bibles
our dining room tabernacle creaking its praise to the father, Ford, &
son, Cadillac

imagine a glacier of freezer burned ham hocks
and Saturday morning's hot-comb exorcism

imagine daddy drunk & speaking tongues, again
dismounting a horse named Excuses in the kitchen

the rice scooped from the church steps
might be the only part of some marriages worth saving

HOUSEQUAKE
880 FWY between San Leandro and San Lorenzo

It was the summer after high school but before eternity.
We were driving down 880 when from the radio
(do I need to explain *radio*?) Housequake began to play.

What happened next I've only seen in church
among its ocean of elders in a bloom of hats
    Even the choir girls said when you're touched just
    right
       it burns holy ghost hot

She was driving but could no longer hold it
      My sister
      My friend
      My confidante
She sped to the next exit
barely peeling off the asphalt for the shoulder
before ejecting herself from the quaking car to dance.
      Just shut up already, damn.

We danced beneath a disco ball of freeway headlights
because the power of Purple compelled us.

THIS is how to get God's attention and company.

Wherever we were going, we had arrived already
We were on fire *running* from water.

And so— here's to the moaning needs of the highway

here to stained backseats and driving a stick uphill with your tongue
here's to blowing harmonics from the source of all sound.

This is something momma can't compute
to call fire by its first name
to dance and know god at the side of the road
purify me in all the things momma told me not to do.

Momma, take a bite of this purple orange
and work your body like a whore.

COMMONALITIES
14th and Mandela Parkway, Oakland

My roommate slash landlord brought to my door
The one guest at his party who wouldn't talk.
Here, he said. Meet him and tossed the freshly caught stranger into my room.

I gave my guest the only chair and set up a chessboard.
Through my now open door, a toddler wandered in—
Jacketed in corduroy, tiny hands, planetary eyes.

My room opened over him like a city; skyscraper ceiling,
a milk crate library threaded with rope lights
a flea market dresser and TV from which Godzilla rampaged.

A woman tiptoed in as if sneaking through a church service
and silently guided the little man out.
She never looked up, he never looked down.

At the end of our game, my guest said: *Where that blunt at?*
After the only refreshment I offered. I fished it from my drawer
and led him through a dining room

full of people
We were invisible to everyone
except the tiny man who pursued us with his eyes.

The back porch. A sparkling black circuit board sky.
We sat and traded commonalities. Coincidences.

Clouds drifted past and we sent sheets of smoke after them.

The sky was so immense you could see it with your whole body.
I realize I'd been here before and say so:
A fishing processor. Alaska. Spring 1995.

I sailed the Bering Sea
chasing herring for money
and earned nothing except fatigue, I said.

I learned to play chess on a ship, he said. Off the coast of Ghana.
Smoke wriggled between his fingers and curled like lace from his mouth.
These African brothers set up a board and played every night.

He and I exchanged what we knew of stars and grids, of ships and types of drowning.
We knitted clouds worthy enough to interweave the sky
We talked until dew flurried and the night stared back at us.

We talked until our fingers fidgeted empty and cold.
We out-talked the party.
It had finished by the time we came in for the night.

Table clear, house silenced. We shook hands.
Two ghosts haunting the same building
Strangers having forgotten we were once brothers,

or vice versa. *Why am I telling you this?*
There are jokes without punchlines.
Stories without endings.

Lives that rhyme and make sense together,
but only once.
Many nights I have been the little man smoking with God, alone

and proposed a chandelier of constellations for the lonely,
those dependent upon celestial navigation and forecasts
That night there was no moon   and no darkness, either.

Just a map without boundaries
A pop-up shop of casual mercies
shaped like love affairs.

Love affairs, like stars, that dazzle only to die
leaving a light that continues to echo
for 100,000 years

THIS PAST SATURDAY AT FARMER'S MARKET
Lakeshore Ave., Oakland

An African brother shoves at us a basket
of boysenberries as if paying a debt. They bleed
on our fingertips, plead sweet mercy on our tongues.
Asked his name, the man smiles proper, his hand a gift,
says: *Too Complicated.*
We buy nine dollars in cherries
off him, all white and red
and spotted and sweet and sour, too. Flavors
turning in our mouths anxious as police lights.
We– no, I—nearly trip over this sister pushing a baby carriage.
We know her, but couldn't pull her name for nothing!
Her new daughter asleep in turtle shell carriage
her cheeks soft as rain-soaked petals.
Her three-year-old son standing sentry
digs into our kettle corn sack only after momma
stamps approval with a glance.

Later: fish tacos for me, Himalayan
curried chicken for her, us both lunching
watching children bounce in the fountain.
Hot-pepper toes pickled cool in water. Giggles
going off like Chinese firecrackers.
Dimples in bloom! Tiny teeth at separate corners
of the mouth grudge-matching. Thighs
you'd want to fried-chicken-bite so golden brown.
Pity another poor momma, her daughter catfish-writhing
on her lap, mango-shake-shook

everywhere! The little girl on a straw
never blinks, channeling opium addict ancestors
thru the unique ecstasy of fruit sugar.

This is us at farmer's market, circling
back to brother Too Complicated who
offers one arm for her, the other for me. A chain
of chins on his shoulders. *Where you been*
he asks double hugging us. And why has
it taken you so long to come back?

Acknowledgments

Lemme Holla At You, and **Ultraviolet** appeared in Zyzzyva #127

Clothesline was published in *The Racket* (March 2o22)

Housequake was published in *A Prince Tribute: I Only Wanted One Time To See You Laughing* edited by Frances Moran (2016)

Preface to A Photograph: 1976 was published by *Alta Journal* (Winter 2021)

Untied appeared in *Patrice Lumumba: An Anthology of Writers on Black Liberation* (2021)

Flirting Phlebotomists published online at *InterlitQ*

Worm's Easter Sunday Monologue appeared in *Colossus: Home Anthology Of Lives In and Out of Place* (2020)

The Florist converts Laurie Anderson's song *White Lily* into a poetic form.

Ghost Homies samples brief phrases from pandemic Youtube live streams of *Dre O.G. Reacts* and *SimbaTV.*

Cave Canem fellow **JAMES CAGNEY** is the award winning author of *Black Steel Magnolias In The Hour Of Chaos Theory* (Black Lawrence Press, 2023) and *MARTIAN: The Saint Of Loneliness* (Nomadic Press, 2022). He was born, raised, and currently resides in Oakland, Ca. Visit his website JamesCagneyPoet.com